His Finest Hour

David Neuhaus

Boulder, Colorado

Book design by NeuStudio Inc.
The text of this book is set in Providence Sans.
The illustrations are rendered in ink and watercolor dyes.

Printed in Hong Kong.

10 9 8 7 6 5 4 3 2 1

Distributed in the United States and Canada by Publishers Group West.

Library of Congress Cataloging-in-Publication Data available
ISBN 1-931382-49-2

VeloPress®
1830 North 55th Street
Boulder, Colorado 80301-2700 USA
303/440-0601; Fax 303/444-6788; E-mail velopress@insideinc.com

To purchase additional copies of this book or other VeloPress books, call 800/234-8356
or visit us on the Web at www.velopress.com

In memory of my parents,
Charles and Virginia Neuhaus

and for
Janet, Pat, Susan, Sophie and Valerie

This is Dudley.

This is Dudley's friend, Ralph.

Dudley and Ralph have been friends for a long time, although sometimes Ralph doesn't play fair.

One day after school, Ralph saw his heroes, the local bicycle racing team, speed by. He dreamed of being asked to join the team, and he thought of a good way to show off. He challenged Dudley to a bicycle race.

The start of the race was the movie theater and the finish was the ice cream stand in the park.

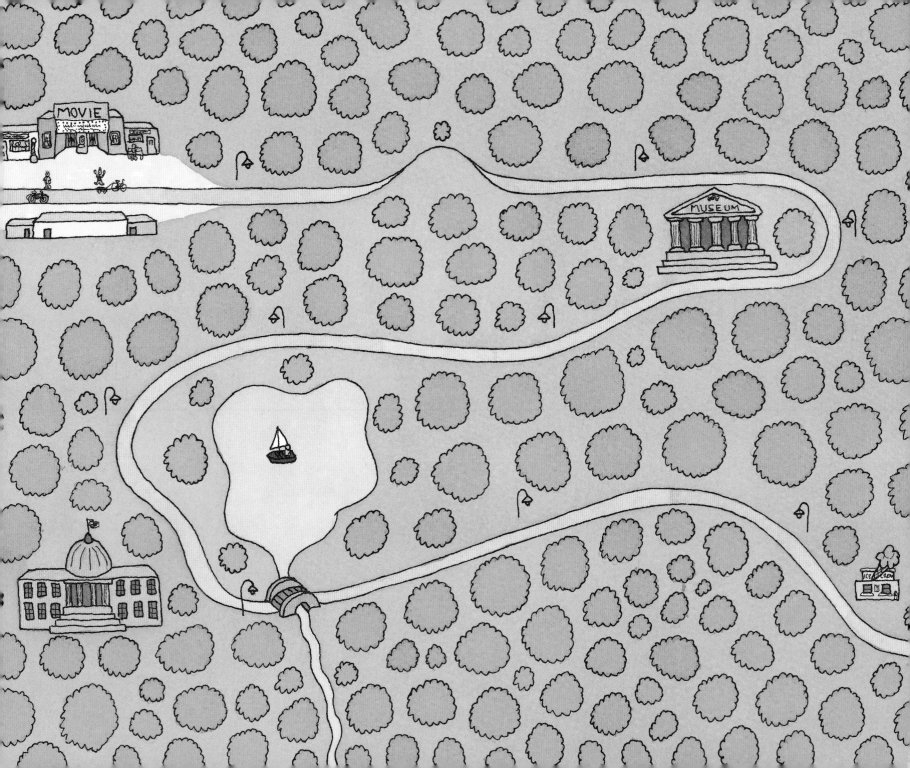

Ralph arrived at the starting line with his bike,
custom-fit biking shoes, cycling gloves,
racing shorts, imported shirt, aerodynamic helmet,
high-pressure pump, imported tools, and water bottle
filled with a special fruit drink for extra energy.

Dudley came with his bike.

When the starting gun was fired, Ralph shifted gears and took off like a bullet.

Soon Ralph was far ahead of Dudley.

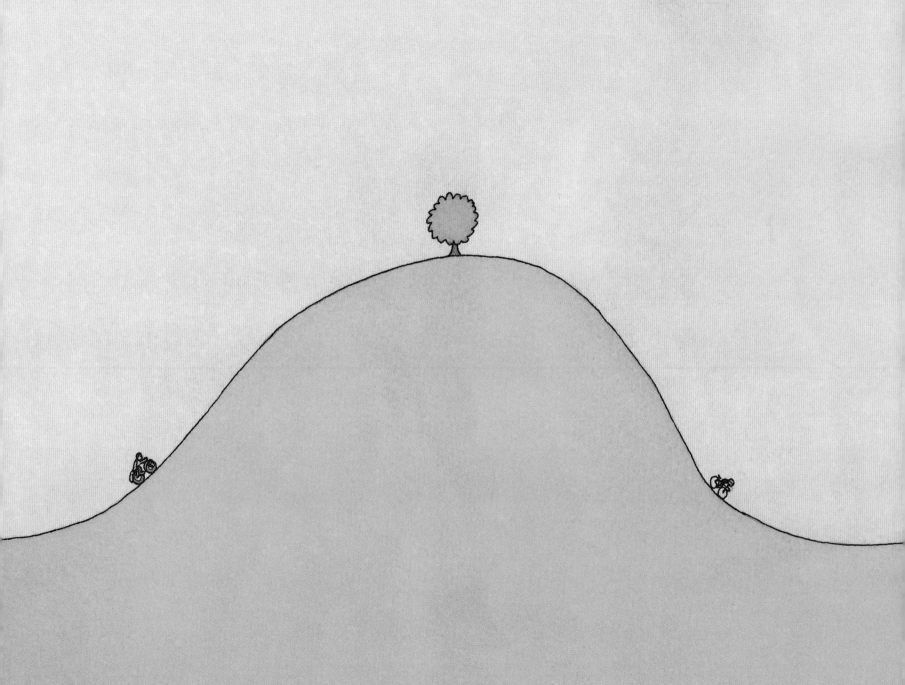

Ralph saw some pretty girls sitting on a park bench. He decided to show off.

Dudley pedaled on. From out of nowhere, the racing team appeared and shouted words of encouragement.

When Ralph realized that Dudley had taken the lead, he decided to use his secret weapon, and he switched on his rocket engine.

Whoosh went the engine.

Z o o m went the bike.

At the last split second, Ralph caught up with Dudley. It was going to be a mighty close race.

Ralph beat Dudley by half an inch.

The crowd applauded Dudley's good sportsmanship and the team captain asked him to join the team. Then the team captain treated everybody to ice cream cones.

Everybody except Ralph, who couldn't be found.

Ralph hoped that his rocket engine
would soon run out of fuel.